BEGINNING PIANO SOLO

Gospel Hymn Favorites

ISBN 978-1-4234-6042-8

HAL•LEONARD®
CORPORATION

7777 W. BLUEMOUND RD. P.O. BOX 13819 MILWAUKEE, WI 53213

Visit Hal Leonard Online at
www.halleonard.com

AT CALVARY

Words by WILLIAM R. NEWELL
Music by DANIEL B. TOWNER

Moderately

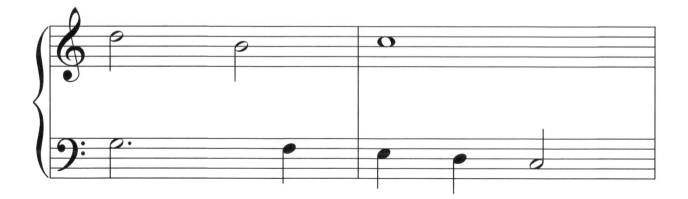

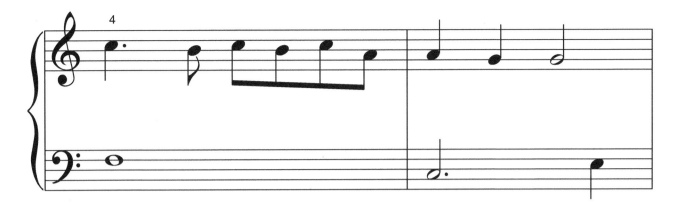

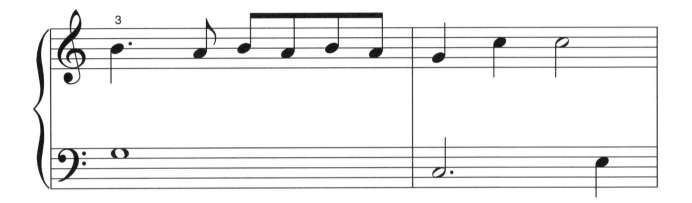

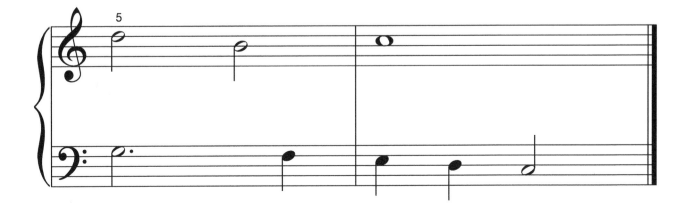

DOWN AT THE CROSS

(Glory to His Name)

Words by ELISHA A. HOFFMAN
Music by JOHN H. STOCKTON

Joyfully

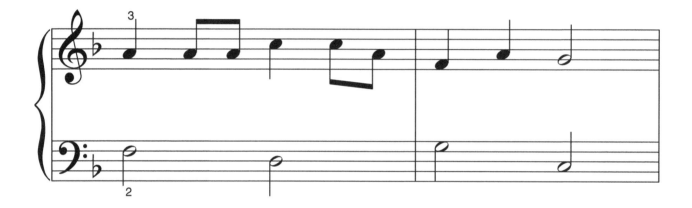

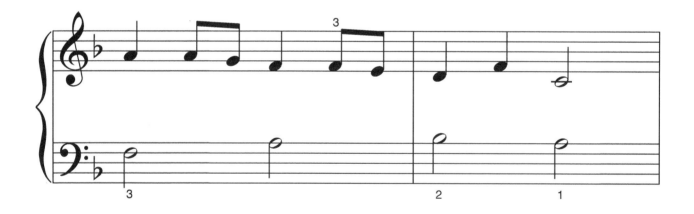

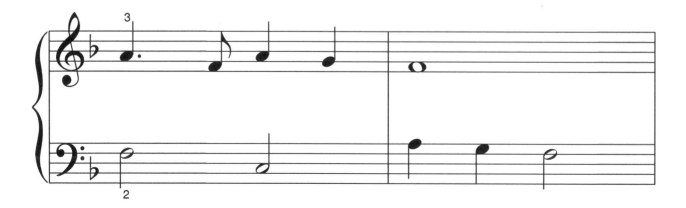

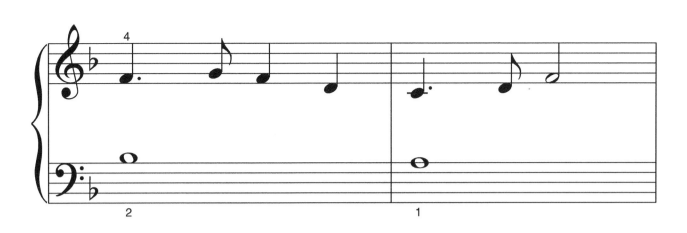

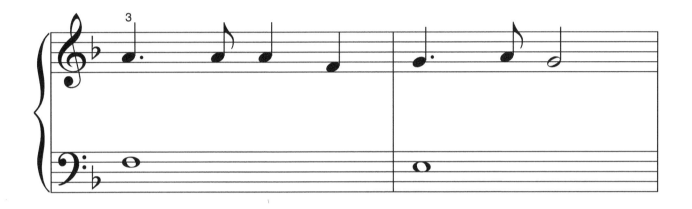

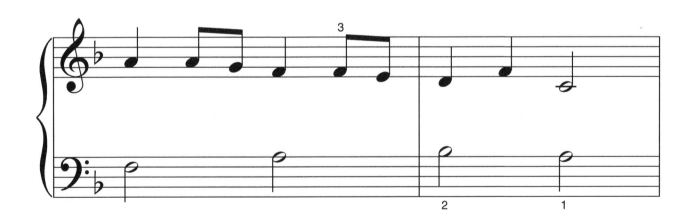

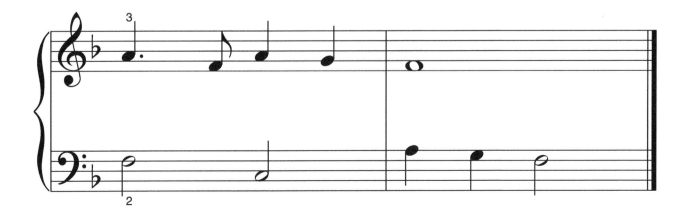

FOOTSTEPS OF JESUS

Words by MARY B.C. SLADE
Music by ASA B. EVERETT

Moderately

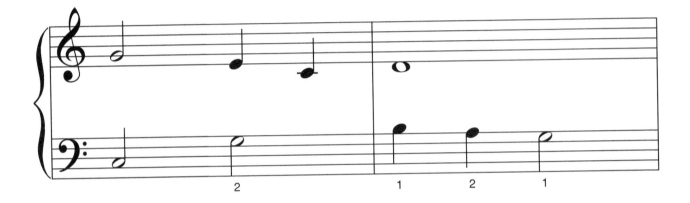

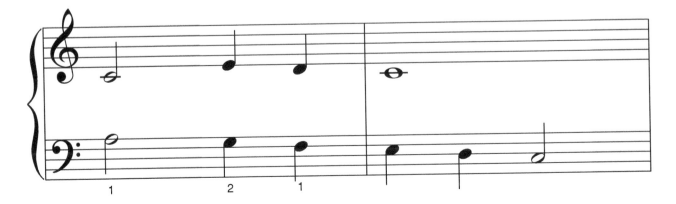

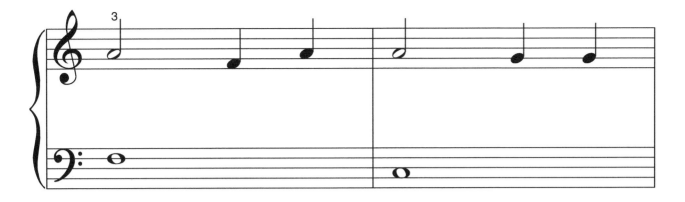

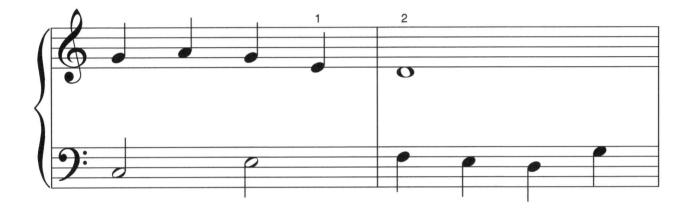

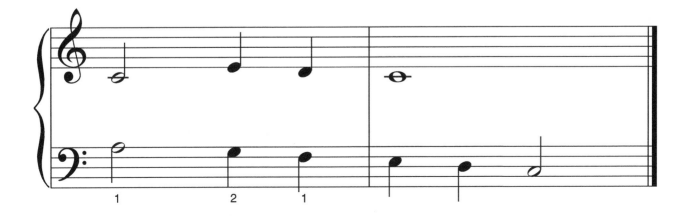

HIS EYE IS ON THE SPARROW

Words by CIVILLA D. MARTIN
Music by CHARLES H. GABRIEL

Warmly

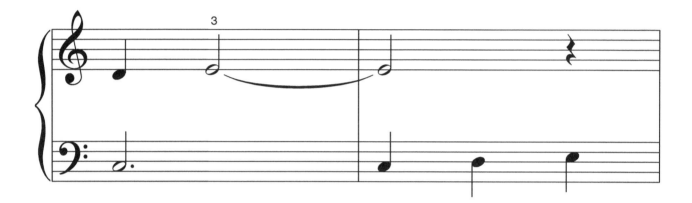

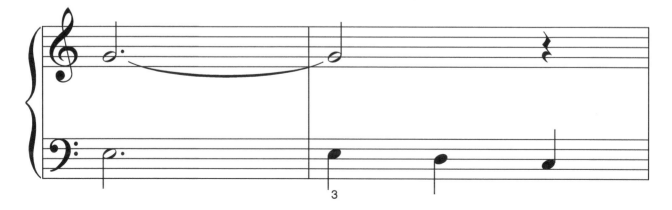

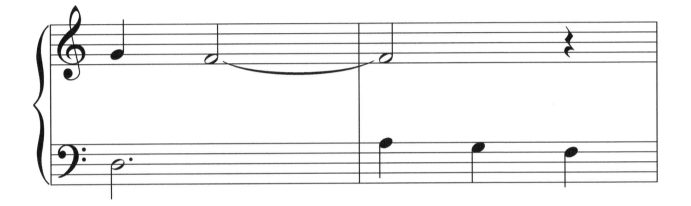

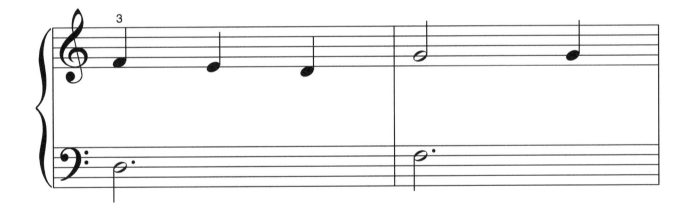

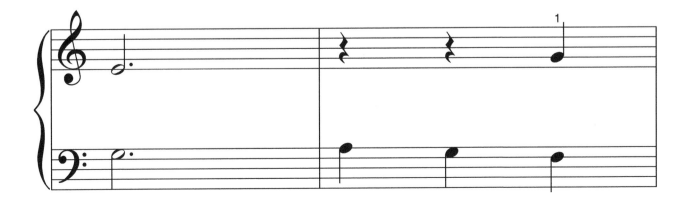

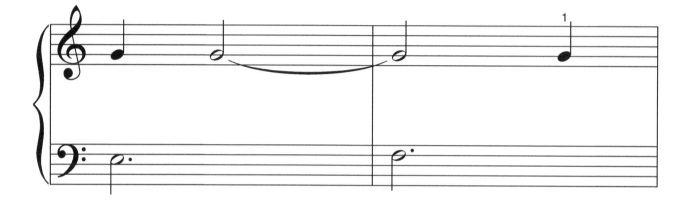

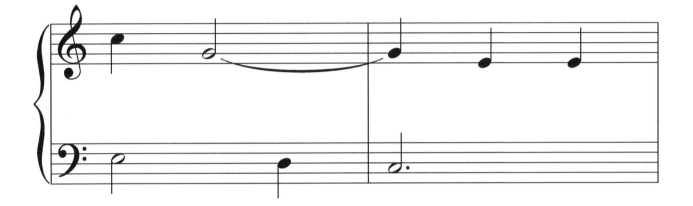

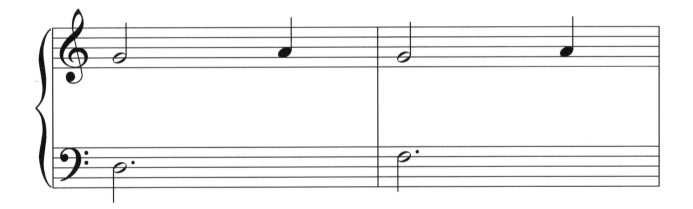

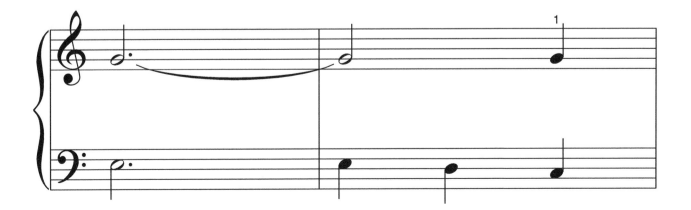

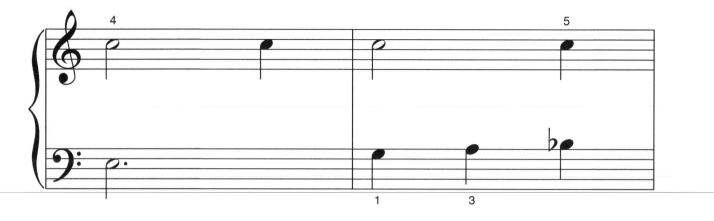

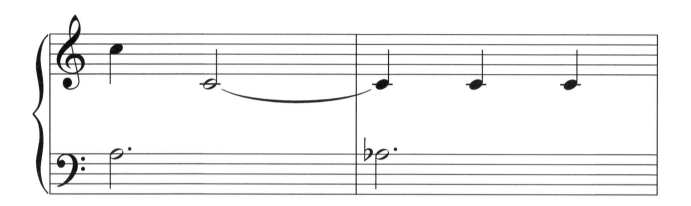

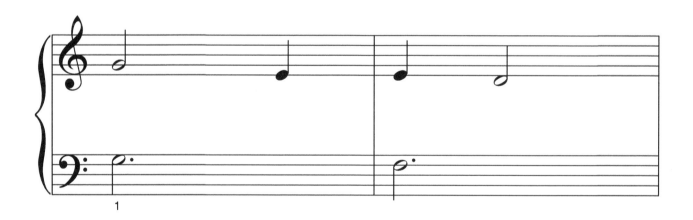

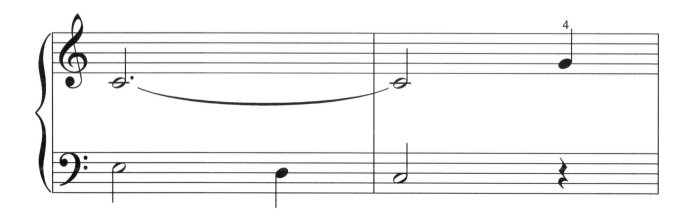

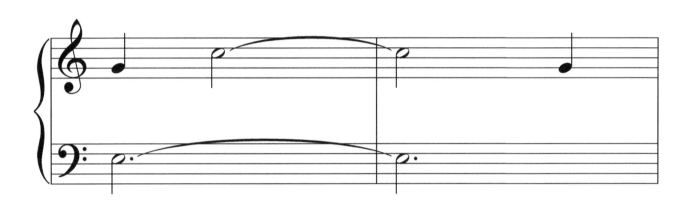

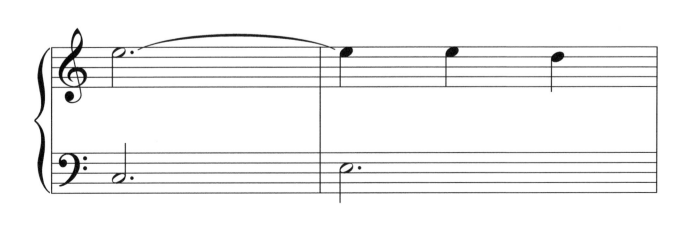

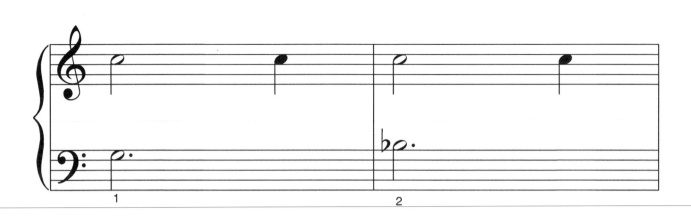

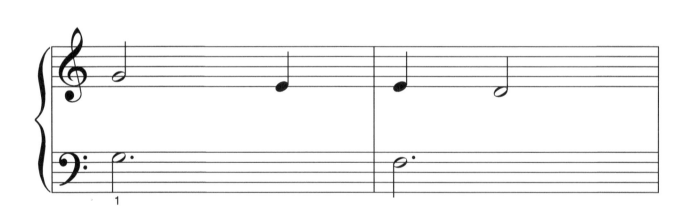

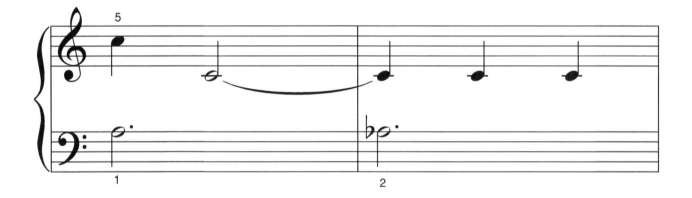

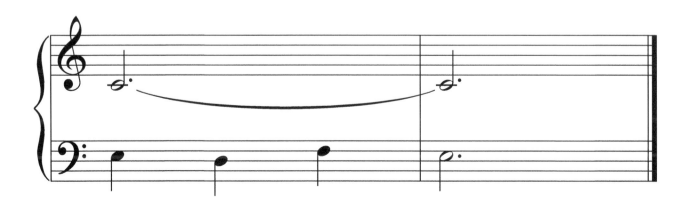

I LOVE TO TELL THE STORY

Words by A. CATHERINE HANKEY
Music by WILLIAM G. FISCHER

Moderately

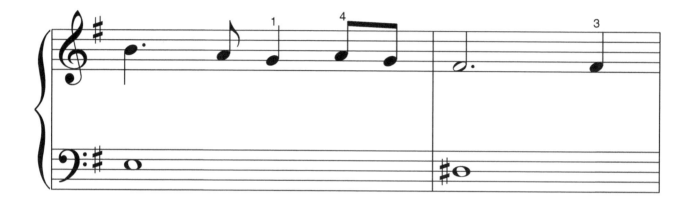

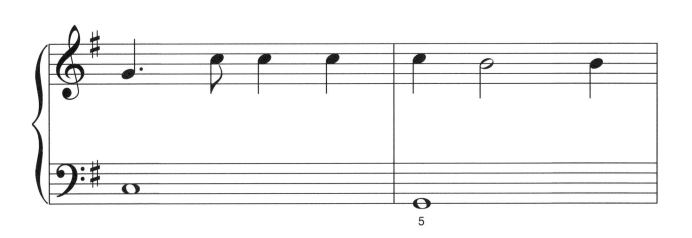

IN THE GARDEN

Words and Music by
C. AUSTIN MILES

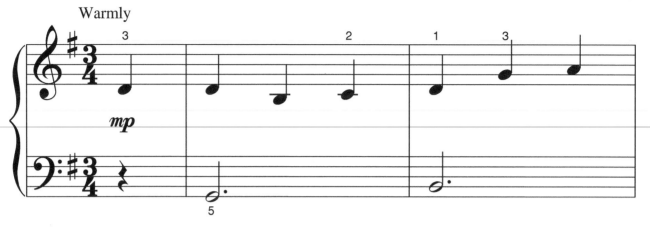

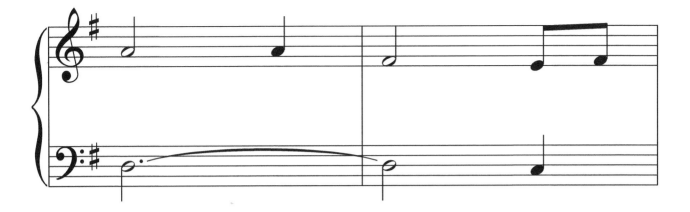

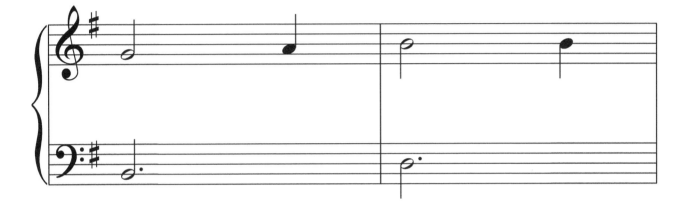

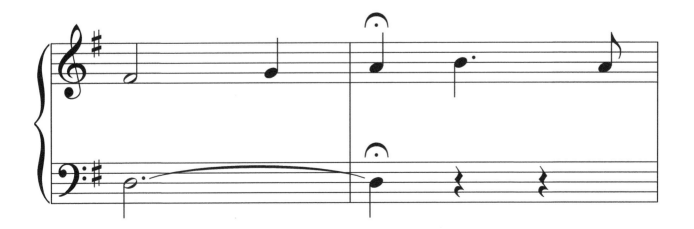

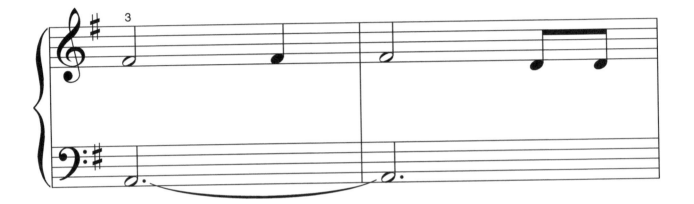

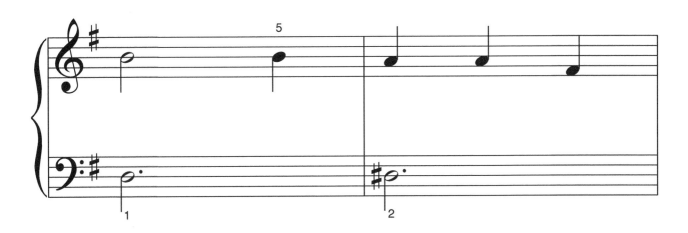

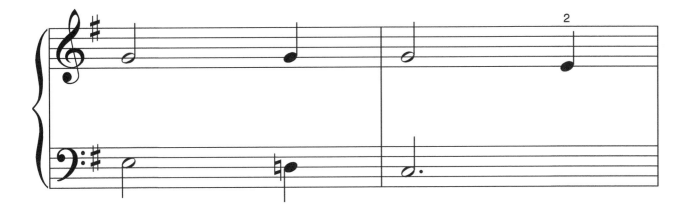

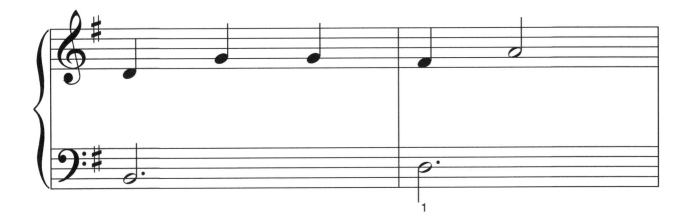

THE OLD RUGGED CROSS

Words and Music by
REV. GEORGE BENNARD

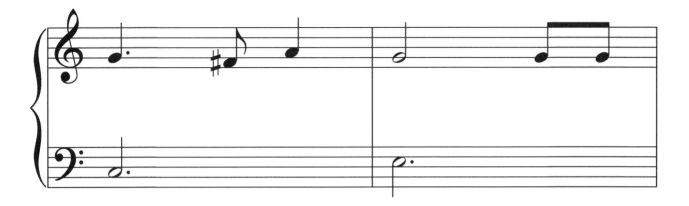

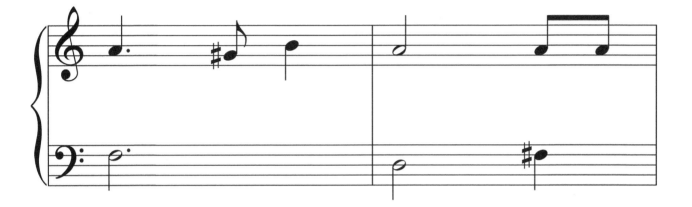

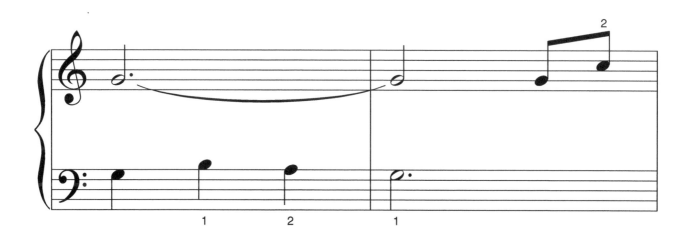

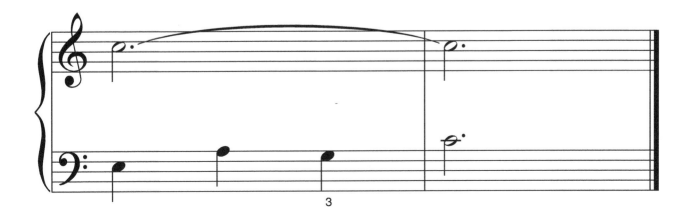

3

THERE IS POWER IN THE BLOOD

Words and Music by
LEWIS E. JONES

Joyfully

WHEN WE ALL GET TO HEAVEN

Words by ELIZA E. HEWITT
Music by EMILY D. WILSON

Moderately

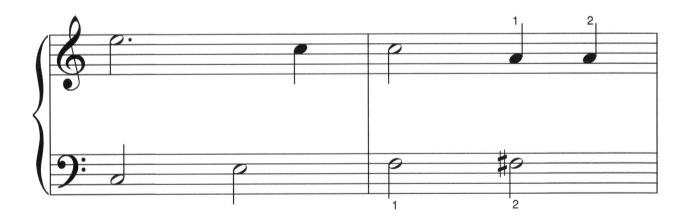

WONDROUS LOVE

Southern American Folk Hymn

Moderately

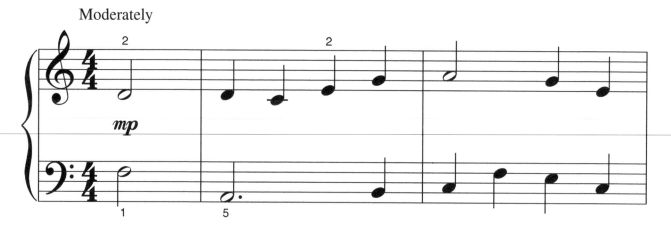

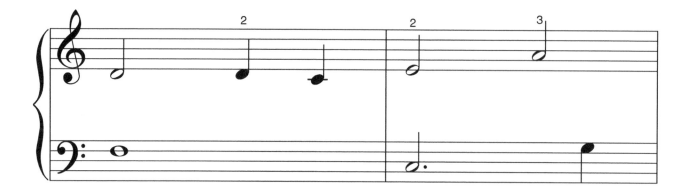

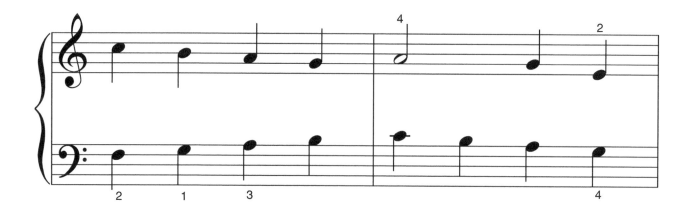

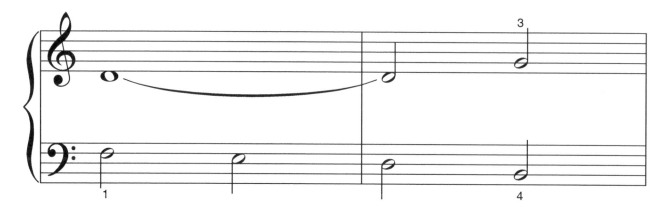

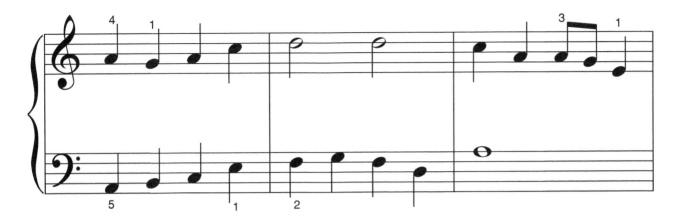

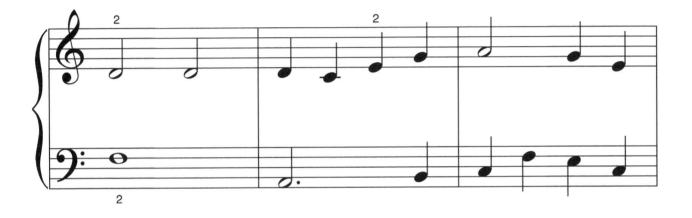

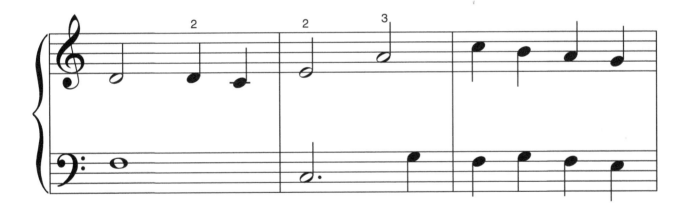

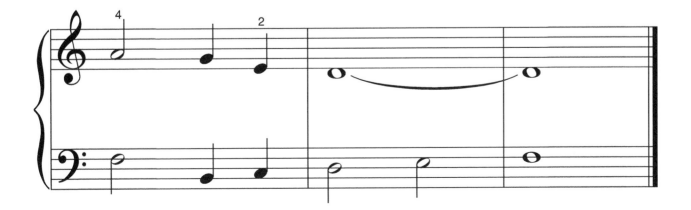

THE BEST SACRED COLLECTIONS FOR PIANO

The Big Book of Hymns

An invaluable collection of 125 favorite hymns, including: All Hail the Power of Jesus' Name • Battle Hymn of the Republic • Blessed Assurance • For the Beauty of the Earth • Holy, Holy, Holy • It Is Well with My Soul • Just as I Am • A Mighty Fortress Is Our God • The Old Rugged Cross • Onward Christian Soldiers • Rock of Ages • Sweet By and By • What a Friend We Have in Jesus • Wondrous Love • and more.

00310510 P/V/G $19.99

The Best Gospel Songs Ever

80 of the best-loved gospel songs of all time: Amazing Grace • At Calvary • Because He Lives • Behold the Lamb • Daddy Sang Bass • His Eye Is on the Sparrow • His Name Is Wonderful • How Great Thou Art • I Saw the Light • I'll Fly Away • Just a Closer Walk with Thee • Just a Little Talk with Jesus • Mansion over the Hilltop • The Old Rugged Cross • Peace in the Valley • Will the Circle Be Unbroken • Wings of a Dove • more.

00310503 P/V/G $19.99

Hymns for Easy Classical Piano

arr. Phillip Keveren

15 beloved songs of faith masterfully presented in a classical style for easy piano. Includes: Abide with Me • A Mighty Fortress Is Our God • Praise God, from Whom All Blessings Flow • in Jesus • Were You There? • and more.

00160294 Easy Piano $12.99

The Christian Children's Songbook

101 songs from Sunday School, all in appropriate keys for children's voices. Includes: Awesome God • The B-I-B-L-E • Clap Your Hands • Day by Day • He's Got the Whole World in His Hands • Jesus Loves Me • Let There Be Peace on Earth • This Little Light of Mine • more.

00310472 P/V/G $19.95

The Hymn Collection

arranged by Phillip Keveren

17 beloved hymns expertly and beautifully arranged for solo piano by Phillip Keveren. Includes: All Hail the Power of Jesus' Name • I Love to Tell the Story • I Surrender All • I've Got Peace Like a River • Were You There? • and more.

00311071 Piano Solo $12.99

P/V/G = Piano/Vocal/Guitar arrangements.
Prices, contents and availability subject to change without notice.

Hymn Duets

arranged by Phillip Keveren

Includes lovely duet arrangements of: All Creatures of Our God and King • I Surrender All • It Is Well with My Soul • O Sacred Head, Now Wounded • Praise to the Lord, The Almighty • Rejoice, The Lord Is King • and more.

00311544 Piano Duet $12.99

Hymn Medleys

arranged by Phillip Keveren

Great medleys resonate with the human spirit, as do the truths in these moving hymns. Here Phillip Keveren combines 24 timeless favorites into eight lovely medleys for solo piano.

00311349 Piano Solo $12.99

Hymns for Two

arranged by Carol Klose

12 piano duet arrangements of favorite hymns: Amazing Grace • Be Thou My Vision • Crown Him with Many Crowns • Fairest Lord Jesus • Holy, Holy, Holy • I Need Thee Every Hour • O Worship the King • What a Friend We Have in Jesus • and more.

00290544 Piano Duet $10.99

Ragtime Gospel Hymns

arranged by Steven Tedesco

15 traditional gospel hymns, including: At Calvary • Footsteps of Jesus • Just a Closer Walk with Thee • Leaning on the Everlasting Arms • What a Friend We Have in Jesus • When We All Get to Heaven • and more.

00311763 Piano Solo $9.99

Seasonal Sunday Solos for Piano

24 blended selections grouped by occasion. Includes: Breath of Heaven (Mary's Song) • Come, Ye Thankful People, Come • Do You Hear What I Hear • God of Our Fathers • In the Name of the Lord • Mary, Did You Know? • Mighty to Save • Spirit of the Living God • The Wonderful Cross • and more.

00311971 Piano Solo $14.99

Sunday Solos for Piano

30 blended selections, perfect for the church pianist Songs include: All Hail the Power of Jesus' Name • Be Thou My Vision • Great Is the Lord • Here I Am to Worship • Majesty • Open the Eyes of My Heart • and many more.

00311272 Piano Solo $16.99

More Sunday Solos for Piano

A follow-up to *Sunday Solos for Piano*, this collection features 30 more blended selections perfect for the church pianist. Includes: Agnus Dei • Come, Thou Fount of Every Blessing • The Heart of Worship • How Great Thou Art • Immortal, Invisible • O Worship the King • Shout to the Lord • Thy Word • We Fall Down • and more.

00311864 Piano Solo $15.99

Even More Sunday Solos for Piano

30 blended selections, including: Ancient Words • Brethren, We Have Met to Worship • How Great Is Our God • Lead On, O King Eternal • Offering • Savior, Like a Shepherd Lead Us • We Bow Down • Worthy of Worship • and more.

00312098 Piano Solo $15.99

Weekly Worship
52 HYMNS FOR A YEAR OF PRAISE
arr. Phillip Keveren

52 hymns that will keep you playing all year long! Each song also includes a brief history by Lindsay Rickard. Hymns include: Abide with Me • All Creatures of Our God and King • Amazing Grace • Be Thou My Vision • It Is Well with My Soul • Just As I Am • The Old Rugged Cross • Savior, like a Shepherd Lead Us • When I Survey the Wondrous Cross • and more.

00145342 Easy Piano $16.99

HAL•LEONARD®

www.halleonard.com